What Is
Martin Luther King, Jr., Day?

By Margot Parker

Illustrated by Matthew Bates

 CHILDRENS PRESS®

CHICAGO

Library of Congress Cataloging-in-Publication Data

Parker, Margot.
    What is Martin Luther King Jr., Day? / by Margot Parker : illustrated
by Matt Bates.
        p.   cm.
    Summary: Describes the life of the civil rights worker who is
honored on Martin Luther King Day.
    ISBN 0-516-03784-2
    1.   Martin Luther King Day—Juvenile literature.   2.   King, Martin
Luther, Jr., 1929-1968—Juvenile literature.   [1.   King, Martin
Luther, Jr., 1929-1968.   2.   Clergy.   3.   Civil rights workers.
4.   Afro-Americans—Biography.   5.   Martin Luther King Day.]
I.   Bates, Matt, ill.   II.   Title.
E185.97.K5P26   1990
323'.092—dc20   89-29254
[B]   CIP
[92]   AC

"Hi, Janet! Hi, Amy! Hi,
Daniel!" Ben shouted.
"Tomorrow is a holiday, and I'm
going ice-skating! Want to
come?"

"Brrrr!" shivered Amy. "I'm going to stay in my warm house."

"No, thank-you," said Daniel. "Janet and I are going to march in a parade."

"A parade? What kind of
parade?" asked Amy.

"Amy, don't you know why we
have a holiday tomorrow?"
asked Janet.

"I think," said Ben, "it's about some king. Oh, I remember now. It's to honor a king named Martin."

"No. It's because we are
honoring a famous man named
Martin Luther King, Jr. He
wasn't a king—but 'King' was
his last name," said Daniel.

"What made him so famous?"
asked Ben.

"Recess is over," said Janet.
"We'd better hurry back to
class."

"But I want to know more about Martin Luther King!" exclaimed Amy.

"So do I," said Ben.

Daniel smiled. "Come over to our house after school, and I'll tell you all about this great man."

"OK! We'll see you later," said Amy.

"When Martin Luther King, Jr., was a little boy," Daniel began, "he lived in a big two-story house in the city of Atlanta, Georgia.

Martin Luther King, Jr. was born in this house in Atlanta, Georgia.

"Martin's father was the minister of the Ebenezer Baptist Church. He taught his children to treat all people fairly.

Ebenezer Baptist Church is in Atlanta.

The King family: Standing from left to right, Alberta Williams King, Martin Luther King, Sr., Mrs. Jennie Williams, Martin's grandmother. Sitting from left to right, Alfred Daniel King, Christine King, and young Martin Luther King, Jr.

"But as Martin grew older, he began to notice that all people were not treated the way his father had taught him.

"He especially noticed that African Americans were treated differently."

"How were black people treated differently?" asked Amy.

"Black people had to use different drinking fountains and different restrooms," replied Daniel.

"Black children could not go to school with white children.

"Black people had to sit in the back of the bus.

Some states had laws that said black people could not sit next to white people on buses.

"They couldn't eat where they
wanted.
"And they couldn't get the
kinds of jobs they wanted.

In college, Martin Luther King, Jr. learned about
Mahatma Gandhi of India. Gandhi (right) did not believe
in violence. He said that people could change laws
by holding peaceful public demonstrations.

"When Martin went to college, he learned about a man from India who said that all people are the same, no matter what they look like. The man from India also believed that people could change unfair laws peacefully.

"Martin also believed this could be done. He had an idea about how he could help change things so that all people would be treated the same.

"Martin's idea was that the change would take place peacefully, without fighting.

"He taught that all people have equal rights to equal treatment under the law," said Daniel.

Public marches and peaceful demonstrations were held throughout the United States.

"What does 'equal' mean?" asked Amy.

" 'Equal' means 'the same'," said Ben.

"And these equal rights are called 'civil rights'," said Daniel.

Martin Luther King, Jr. (left) and the Reverend Ralph Abernathy (right) led many civil rights marches.

"Dr. King and other black leaders worked hard to change the laws.

"So Dr. King led peaceful marches in many cities where laws needed changing.

Coretta Scott King (above) marched with her husband Martin. In Alabama, thousands of people joined Dr. King on the march from Selma to Montgomery.

"In August 1963, Dr. King led the biggest civil rights march of all to Washington, D.C., the capital of the United States of America.

"When he stood before the great crowd, he said, 'I have a dream today. I have a dream that one day...black boys and black girls will be able to join hands with...white boys and white girls and walk together as sisters and brothers.'

Thousands gathered in front of the Lincoln Memorial in Washington, D. C. and heard Dr. King deliver his famous "I Have a Dream" speech.

"Many Americans agreed with Dr. King, but some did not. They tried to keep him from leading the marches.

"Sometimes Dr. King became discouraged. But he decided to keep on working for his dream.

"In December of 1964, he was honored by being given the Nobel Peace Prize."

Dr. Martin Luther King, Jr. was awarded
the Nobel Peace Prize in 1964.

"What's the Nobel Peace
Prize?" asked Ben.

"It is a large amount of
money given to someone who
has worked hard for peace,"
answered Daniel.

"Dr. King did not keep the
prize money. He gave it to
some other people who had
worked with him for peace.

"He continued to go to other cities to help black people gain their rights.

"In April 1968, he went to Memphis, Tennessee, to help get better working conditions for the city's garbage collectors.

This photograph showing Dr. King standing on the balcony of his Memphis motel was taken the day before Dr. King was shot. From left to right: Hosea Williams, Jesse Jackson, Dr. King, and Ralph Abernathy

"One evening while he was in Memphis, Dr. King stepped outside his motel room.

"A man who hated him was hiding across the street with a rifle. When the man saw Dr. King, he shot and killed him.

A farm wagon pulled by two mules was used to carry the coffin of
Dr. Martin Luther King, Jr. More than 50,000 people attended
Dr. King's funeral in Atlanta, Georgia.

"Many people in America who loved Dr. King found it hard to believe that someone had killed him.

"They wanted to help continue his dream by remembering his birthday as a national holiday.

This simple headstone marks Dr. King's grave. Martin Luther King, Jr. was born in 1929. He died in 1968. The man who killed Dr. King was sentenced to ninety-nine years in prison.

"It took a long time, but fifteen years after he died, Congress voted to begin this holiday in 1986."

"Martin Luther King's birthday
is on January 15," said Janet,
"but each year we celebrate it
on the third Monday in
January."

"Just think," Ben said, "if Dr. King had not worked so hard, we might not be going to the same school. And you might not be my friend."

"Dr. King did a lot," said Daniel.
"But there are still many people
who don't like other people
because they are different. We
still have work to do."